From a New Forest Inclosure

Book Two 2006 & 2007

By

Ian Thew

Published by Burley Rails Publishing
Burley Rails Cottage BH24 4HT

ISBN 978-0-9570835-1-6

Ian Thew

Born in Southampton, Ian and his siblings were brought, throughout their childhood, into the New Forest to walk and enjoy the open space. Although, initially, he spent his adult life living and working away from the Forest he was always keen on the countryside and country sports, especially fishing and shooting. He returned whenever he could to the Forest until, eventually, he settled down in Burley with his late wife, Diane. In 1994 they moved to the remote Burley Rails Cottage which, originally built as a woodman's cottage and sold by the Forestry Commission in the 1960's, is a unique place in which to live.

Ian's knowledge of the forest is genuine and he is respected for his considerate and well researched articles which are published in national and international magazines.

These booklets have been produced with the encouragement of readers who wished to refer to a particular article which had been lost in a discarded magazine and at the suggestion of those who wanted friends, relatives and visitors in general to understand the Forest and its ways. So whether a Villager, Visitor, Tourist, or Grockle, whatever your guise, we hope these snippets will help you to understand what is so very special about this wonderful place.

'From a New Forest Inclosure The First Two Years' received such kind reviews that it was not a difficult decision to continue in the same vein and publish this volume, 'From a New Forest Inclosure Book Two 2006 & 2007', which is a compilation of the original articles written for the Burley Village magazine, during that period.

The book has been further enhanced by the inclusion of eighteen original colour photographs.

The subject matter is varied; sometimes serious, always informative and often amusing. So why don't you delve into these pages and discover the spider that walks on water, the Iceman, sea trout, wild fungi, the Drift and much, much more.

Ian Thew

January

By the time you read this the year 2005 will be just a memory and we will soon forget the recent festivities and begin to look forward to the coming year. So far this winter has proved to be more severe than the previous one and it is cheering on a bleak, raw day to reassure oneself that it won't be too long before the first bird-song will be heard as the early nesters begin preparing for their hungry broods. Not long after this the first migrant visitors will begin to arrive for their summer sojourn and unfortunately, with Easter as a curtain call, the flightless summer visitors will also begin their invasion. I'm talking, of course, about our tourists, campers and holidaymakers. Generally, they are nice people and they are of great benefit to the local economy and now that we are a National Park they have every right to come here. But tell me, if you can, why must some, and I'm sure that these are the minority, leave so much rubbish behind? I walk my dogs every day and I'm no longer surprised by what we find; paper, polythene, glass and plastic bottles, cans, disposable barbeques and even, on one occasion, a roast, shoulder of lamb (the dogs didn't complain about that). I wonder at the mentality of those who can take the trouble to bring a full package or bottle into the Forest but can't be bothered to take away the empty, lighter container, when finished.

I've got other visitors, at the moment, but these are not so welcome. Wood mice have moved into the workshop and have subsequently chewed a large hole in the peanut drum. I was unaware of their presence until one day, I noticed that the Jack Russell was staring intently at my tool box and cocking his head to one side in typical terrier fashion. I carefully opened the lid and there among the pliers and screw drivers in the top tray was a fair sized heap of peanuts which could only have been carried there by a mouse. The Jack examined them with his nose and became very agitated. I gently raised the tray and there, trembling in the tools below, was the mouse. As the dog lunged forward the mouse leapt from the tool box and disappeared under the work bench. The terrier yelped with delight and was instantly joined by the other two dogs and together, the three of them scraped and scratched frantically among the boxes under the bench. Did they catch the mouse?

No, they did not and so far neither have I, but it will have to go, because subsequent mouse-hunts by the dogs have left my workshop looking like the wreck of the Hesperus and my peanut bill is escalating rapidly!

There is another resident mouse that I can't help but admire. About fifteen feet from the kitchen window a peanut feeder hangs from a stout batten that is, in turn, nailed to the top of a six foot high, timber, fence post.

Nuthatch

Recently, I noticed what I thought at first to be an odd looking bird on the feeder. Closer examination revealed a busy little wood mouse who was industriously teasing a peanut through the wire. I watched it for a while and then decided that enough was enough. I opened the door and as soon as I approached the feeder the mouse let go; it fell at least five feet and hit the ground without suffering any injury and scuttled off into the shrubbery. I foolishly thought that that was the last I would see of that rodent. How wrong could I be? It has become a regular visitor and all the birds are afraid of it. When the mouse is hanging on their feeder the finches and tits queue-up on the fence wire like a load of frightened children and wait for it to finish. There is one brave soul however who will not be deprived of its meal and that is the nuthatch. This smart little bird with his blue-grey jacket and buff waistcoat hurls himself without fear at the unwelcome visitor who, in turn, falls to the ground and disappears under the plants. Once the nuthatch has managed to extricate a nut for itself and has flown off, the little mouse scampers up the fence post, over the batten and then onto the peanut basket and there he will remain until once again, he is dive-bombed by the offended nuthatch and falls to the ground below. This routine can continue far longer than I have time to watch but I cannot fail to admire the tenacity of this little mouse and the indignant courage of the nuthatch. I must go now before I drive you all nuts!

Happy New Year

February

It's mid January, and on a mild day like today when the sun is filtering through the bare trees to cast warming patches on the leaf-covered forest floor, you can almost smell the spring around the corner. It's true that we've had, so far, a colder winter than recent years and there's plenty of time left to suffer even greater hardship. One of the coldest days was the first Thursday after Christmas; I awoke to a sharp, white frost and decided that it would be a good day to venture out onto the open plains and valleys to the north of the A31; it's interesting country and quite undisturbed in places and the freezing temperature would make walking across the quaking mires a little easier and at the same time minimise the chance of sinking up to the knees in the peaty hollows between the tussock grasses.

As I closed the gate to my home here in the Inclosure I was amazed to hear a great-spotted woodpecker (or 'woodpie' to give it its Forest name), drumming on one of the nearby trees. I stopped and listened, not sure that on such a bitterly cold day my aged hearing hadn't let me down. But sure enough, there it was again, a brief staccato that echoed through the Forest; a sound that is, to me, a true harbinger of spring. This drumming is made by both sexes who hammer repeatedly on a dead bough or pole to proclaim to all that this is their territory. I waited a while longer, ignoring the eager dogs, and enjoying a sound that hadn't been heard for several months. Finally we set off and walked through a desolate and empty Forest, nothing moved, and nothing but the increasing roar of the traffic as we approached the dual carriageway across Sandy Ridge, assailed our frozen ears. Every creature, it seemed, had fled from this cold and heartless landscape.

Once through the underpass we descended into the first of the valley mires and as we picked our way across the frost-crusted bogs the noise from the smelly road began to diminish. A thick stand of gorse, bright with yellow flowers, lit-up the otherwise drab heather and tussock grasses and suddenly, without warning, a roe doe together with her nearly full-grown kid bounced out from the warm shelter of the spiky bushes and headed for a distant plantation. In the few sparse, grassy bottoms that we encountered one or two desultory ponies raised their heads as we passed by. Perhaps they were questioning our sanity for being in such an unfriendly spot on such a raw day, I know I was! We had struggled through heavy country for more than an hour and not a pigeon, crow or buzzard had been seen when, without warning, from under a clump of skeletal willow trees, through which a meagre trickle of unfrozen water headed towards the far distant sea, a pair of woodcock jinked away on silent wings. These little game birds had found one of the few spots of penetrable ground in this frozen waste where they were able to probe, with their long beaks, for their life sustaining insects and worms. We watched them as they flew on jerky wings across the heather and were pleased to see them land in a similar clump of willows in a neighbouring bottom where, I am sure, they would have found another frost-free runnel in which to feed.

We decided to head for home and our route took us back along part of the stream that had recently been re-routed under the Life 3 project and, to my

Herring Gull

surprise, it was frozen over from one bank to the other. I had never seen this stream frozen before and so with the cold weather in mind and because of the dearth of bird life on the Forest I set off for a spot that I knew would be free of ice --- the sea shore. In fact I ventured in an easterly direction and just poked my nose into Sussex where the sheltered, food-rich harbours are renowned worldwide as winter feeding grounds for many species of birds. My choice of location had not been wrong, and as I walked down a raised, narrow path towards the shore, the marshes on either side of me were bustling with hundreds of widgeon who, regardless of my proximity, were industriously gleaning whatever food they could find in the nutritious, shallow splashes. The harbour waters were as calm as a mill-pond and a good distance from the shore hundreds of birds formed a huge raft on the flat surface. I raised my binoculars and discovered tufted ducks in their elegant black and white jackets together with dark bellied Brent geese and an assortment of seagulls. I walked further along the sea wall and as I idly watched a snowy-white egret that flapped inelegantly towards the shelter of the reed-beds I was conscious of a quiet, repetitive clicking sound. After much deliberation I decided that the sound was coming from a diminutive shingle beach which was curled in an arm of the harbour. To my delight, the binoculars revealed a bustling flock of well camouflaged turnstones. These tiny waders are named after their feeding method and the clicking noise was the sound of each stone as, one after another, they industriously turned them over in search of any food that might be hidden beneath.

So take a tip, if it's cold and frosty and you want to see some birds—go to the seaside.

I'd better go now so you too can turn over!

March

At last, a drop of February rain has plucked up the courage to try and drive away the recent cold and frosty weather and the effect on the birds, in and around the garden, is amazing. The nut and seed feeders no longer need to be filled each and every day which is a sure sign that, as the weather warms up, the birds are beginning to find more of their natural food. Cock fighting seems to have become popular among some of our male birds and the tussles can, sometimes, be so intense that it's possible to walk quite close to these antagonists before they take fright; indeed, my cocker spaniel has, in the last week, presented me with both a wren and a song thrush that, apart from being a little sodden, were completely unharmed and I feel sure that this geriatric dog was only able to capture them because their minds were on other things.

The members of the dawn chorus are beginning to tune-up and every morning provides a slightly better performance than the one before. The wood peckers are, by now, giving regular and more prolonged drumming instructions and the odd wood pigeon has been observed in courtship flight. As I look out from my study a tiny treecreeper is working its way up the trunk of a substantial old oak. It will be looking for insects hidden in the crevices in the bark which it will winkle out with its delicate but sharp and curved beak. Its method of progress is to hop, with both feet at once, up the trunk and, gripping with its long claws and using its stiff tail as a prop it makes it way in a spiralled route around and up the trunk. It is, however, impossible for the treecreeper to travel down the tree in this fashion so you will observe that, once it has satisfied itself that it has gleaned all it can from a particular tree, it will fly to the base of another, adjacent trunk and from there, start its vertical food search once again.

There have been some interesting birds reported recently. Among others, great grey shrikes have been spotted on the Forest. These birds with their black, white and grey plumage and distinctive black eye band feed on small birds, mammals and insects and their habit of impaling their victims on thorns or barbed wire, for later consumption, has earned them the nickname of "butcher birds". Ravens are becoming more numerous and this largest member of the British crow family is easily distinguished by its shear size and its kronking call. There was one perched in a tree-top by Gods Gate a few days ago and it was possible to see the raised feathers on its crown and throat each time it bowed to give a croak. My friend, Brian who lives at Bashley, takes great delight, each year, to call and let me know that the siskins have arrived on his bird tables. Sure enough, last week he rang to tell me that he had about twenty with him already and why these charming, canary coloured finches should arrive at his feeders long before they get to me, I'll never understand. His other news was the sighting of a small group of crossbills. These are striking little birds, the male has orange-red plumage and the female is dressed in yellow-green and as their name suggests their upper and lower mandibles are crossed over each other, this is to enable them to extract the seeds, on which they feed, from the cones of various species of conifers.

Keep an eye out as you wander round this beautiful part of the world and if you're lucky you may well see some of these rarer birds as well as the more common but no less fascinating varieties --- and oh yes, seen any frogspawn yet? Keep your eyes peeled.

Must hop off now.

Mandarin Drake

April

The early spring colours are now in evidence. Have you noticed the hazel catkins this year? I don't ever recall seeing them look so vibrant nor so lengthy. Near to the bridge over Blackensford brook they hang, up to three inches long, either singly, in pairs or in bunches of three like Christmas decorations over the water, Sadly, at the time of writing this they are beginning to go over and are now looking rather sad; the bright yellow has faded to an insipid green and they will eventually turn brown and fall to the ground. Further along the river bank the alders are sporting their new purple catkins. Where length is concerned, these cannot compete with the hazel but their colour is equally welcome at this time of the year. No more than inch in length these catkins hang in bunches of three, four and five and for a very short time they clothe the trees in a purple haze. Similarly, look for plantations of young silver birch trees and you will be delighted by the purple hue that seems to hang over them.

I know from the enumerable telephone calls that I've received just lately from many Burley residents that, this year, the grey squirrels are raiding their bird tables and feeders with a vengeance. The reason for this is the lack of natural food in some areas. The chestnut and acorn crops were not up to much last autumn and the beech mast was, in my area, non-existent and so the little varmints are bound to seek alternative food sources. Walk through any deciduous woodland at the moment and you'll see very little squirrel activity, but venture among the conifers and pines and you'll find a different story. Look for the stumps of felled trees and you'll almost certainly find them covered in the cores of eaten cones, for these stumps are the squirrel's dining tables and they have, this year, moved en-masse to the coniferous plantations (and to your bird tables) where there is a ready supply of food. I don't get much trouble with the squirrels up here until my weeping willow comes into bud and then they come scuttling over the garage roof and into the tree. Here, one or more of these grey marauders will haul up one of the long, trailing branches and after nibbling a few buds from it will drop it onto the lawn below and then haul up another. They are very destructive and create an awful mess on the grass.

I had some new arrivals in the garden last week. I was having an evening walk around the paddock with the dogs when a pair of mallard executed a low, fly-past over the trees. I hurried under the overhanging roof of the stables and waited; a few minutes later they appeared once more over the beeches and, with much quacking, the drake came swooping into the garden pond. His dowdy little mate almost made it too but at the last minute she applied her air brakes and then rocketed away before she'd touched the water. I've no doubt that she'd spotted the dogs or me and decided that there might be a safer haven elsewhere in which to spend the night. I was a little disappointed to watch the drake take to the air and follow her; I had always hoped that wild ducks might take-up residence on the pond and apart from a pair of mandarin who paid me a visit some years ago, my hopes had never been fulfilled. Imagine my surprise when, the next morning, I looked out from my bedroom window and there, on the pond, were the pair of ducks. They had come in after dark and proceeded to spend the rest of the day either tucked up on the bank or up-ended in the water. That evening I filled a bowl with barley and approached the pond with care. The ducks took flight when I was within about twenty feet of them and so I scattered the corn in and around the margins of the pond and returned to the house. The next morning there was no sign of the birds and I was saddened by their absence until later that morning, when I went to inspect the pond for frog spawn, I noticed that the best part of the barley had gone. I was delighted by this observation and immediately scattered another good helping of food around the pond. I was convinced that the ducks had returned for a feed during the night my vision of a future with multi-coloured birds on the pond was dashed when, an hour or so later, I happened to look out from the conservatory and there, eating the food with great relish, were not the pretty ducks but two big, black crows. Like the squirrels it hadn't take long for these sharp-eyed opportunists to find the bounty I had left and I was sure then that it was they who had mopped-up the previous feed and not the ducks!

Have a very happy Easter

May

I'm pleased to be able to report that my wild mallard ducks have returned, or I should say they can be heard returning each day just after nightfall.
Their arrival is always heralded by some communicative quacking which is soon followed by a discrete splash as each bird makes a safe landing n the water. Sometimes they are still there at day break and have become quite used to both me and the dogs, provided we don't go too close. Every day, when they are away on duck business, I scatter a little barley onto the water margins and it always disappears during the night. The two resident crows are a bit miffed because I'm now feeding the corn into the water instead of onto the banks, but these remarkably intelligent birds still manage, without getting their feet wet, to reach some of the food.
I regret that I mentioned to you in last month's issue that the local squirrels make an annual visit to my weeping willow tree, for I had no sooner emailed the copy to our editor and there they were! I couldn't believe my eyes, there in the uppermost branches were three of the little devils and the lawn below was already strewn with part eaten willow wands. I'm afraid they'll have to go and I just wish, as he does too, that my Jack Russell could climb trees. He now spends a good part of the day staring into the willow from below and I'm sure that he sometimes prays to his doggy God that one of the varmints might slip and fall. It's a wonder he doesn't get a stiff neck!
I had a new find recently. A friend was giving me a tour of a small, private nature reserve on the edge of the Forest when he pointed out a strange looking fungus which was hanging down, rather like a stubby elephant trunk, from the bole of a goat willow. I took some photos and showed them to my fungi mentor who confirmed our suspicions that this was a specimen of the Hoof or Tinder fungus (Fomes formentarius). This is a perennial fungus which is quite common in Scotland and Northern England but unusual in these parts. The name Hoof fungus makes sense because the hard horny outer layer is concentrically ringed by each successive season of growth and in reality it does look like a horse's hoof; albeit one that desperately needs the ministrations of a farrier! The alternative name of Tinder fungus prompted some research which revealed a versatile plant that has been in the service of man for many thousands of years.

The earliest record of this fungus that I could find referred to The Iceman or Oetzi an extremely well preserved Neolithic man who, some 5000 years after his demise, was discovered in 1991 entombed in a glacier near the Austrian/Italian border. In his pouch, among other things, was a small piece of felt-like substance together with several sharpened flints and some slender bone tools.

Hoof or Tinder Fungus (Fomes formentarius)

It was decided, by those who are knowledgeable in the subject, that the flints and bone tools were used for making fire and, after testing the small piece of felt, they declared it to be a piece of Tinder fungus. Since Oetzi's time there are many instances on record of this association with fire. Below the horny exterior of the fungus there is a suede-like layer which has been known for years for its ability to catch fire at the slightest excuse and to continue smouldering steadily for an extremely long time. It is from this characteristic that the name Tinder fungus is derived and, as well as being used as an extremely efficient fire lighter, it was also used to transfer fire from one location to another.

Further investigation and probing on the internet turned up some more uses for Fomes formentarius which must surely be the most useful of all the inedible fungi.   In more recent years than poor old Oetzi the horny outer shell has, in some countries, been hollowed out and hung from a wall to serve as an unusual and decorative planter.   The suede-like material mentioned above can also be used in the manufacture of caps and other items of clothing. It has been used in its unflattened and dry state as a pin cushion which prevented needles and pins from rusting and similarly, early entomologists used it as a medium on which to mount their captured insects. For centuries it has been used in medicine in a variety of ways; as a cauterisation substance in the fifth century, as a styptic by early surgeons and barbers, ad as a remedy for such ailments as haemorrhoids, constipation and cancer.   It has also been smoked and sniffed, down the years, by various tribes and cultures in religious and ritualistic ceremonies. But for me, the most interesting fact about the hoof fungus that I turned up was that it's the source of 'Amadou' and those of you in the village who fly fish, and I know that there are quite a few of you out there, will know all about this product. For the non-fishers 'amadou' is a felt like substance that is used by fly fishermen to dry their flies and very effective it is too, and although its' expensive to buy, it will last for many years.

Now, that reminds me, fishing starts in a few days' time so I must go and check my gear.

                                                            Tight lines.

June

The past two days have been absolute scorchers and all around the Forest is bursting with new life. From my study window I have, all winter, been able to look down the length of a grassy ride that separates a broad leaf enclosure from a Douglas fir plantation but, almost overnight, that vista is gone. A mature oak tree, just beyond the fence, has opened its first leaves and at the same time has produced masses of pendulous flowers. The weight of both the foliage and flowers has lowered the branches to such a degree that my view down the ride is now non-existent. But I don't mind, it's a sure sign that spring is giving way to summer and every day brings a new delight.

The oak flowers remind me of a nest that was built two years ago above the door of an outbuilding by a pair of spotted fly-catchers. It was constructed entirely from oak tree flowers and took them just a day to complete! It was an exquisite example of just how clever and industrious some birds can be. I'm sorry to report that despite the abundance of both nesting material, and food in the form of flies, there's been no sign, so far, of these endearing little birds. They didn't turn up last year either and were sorely missed. I do hope they arrive this season; there's still time and central Africa is a long way for tiny wings!

The mallards on the pond have become quite tame and usually come for their food at about six o'clock in the evening. The drake is usually the first to arrive and his silent arrival is only marred by a slight splash as he lands on the water. After a quick feed, he will sit, resplendent in his brilliant plumage, to await the arrival of 'The Missus' and we certainly know it when she arrives! It's the mallard ducks that make the all too familiar 'quack'. (the drakes have a much weaker, rasping call) and this lady certainly likes to let you know that she's around. She can, without fail, be heard from some distance as she approaches the garden and, quite often, she'll attempt a touch-down on the lawn instead of on the water, which usually results in the duck-equivalent of a crash landing. After such a disaster, she'll pick herself up and, with an indignant waggle of her tail, she'll shout and holler at her poor mate, no doubt blaming him for her recent predicament.

But more recently, she's had something else to shout about; their peaceful existence has been shattered by the arrival of some colourful Asian invaders; a few weeks ago a pair of mandarin ducks had the cheek to gate-crash their European cousins' party. Needless to say, this gave way to outrage on the part of the mallards and, with much quacking and flapping Mrs Mallard saw them both off whilst her hubby sat and watched. But her victory was short-lived, for the next evening the mandarins returned mob-handed; not one, but three gaudy drakes, accompanied by two more sombre ducks, arrived to show them who were the bosses – and then the fun began. Mandarins are perching ducks and they quite happily landed, much to the indignation of the incumbents, in the trees above the pond and on top of the adjacent fence posts. Now this flummoxed the mallards, especially Mrs Mallard who, quacking vociferously, waddled up and down below them. But the mandarins were not fazed by all this bravado and gradually, they took it in turn to drop onto the pond for a feed, but at each attempt they were attacked by the territorial mallards, and some exciting ducky punch-ups ensued, with both contestants coming off about even. After several evenings of heated arguments and heavy loss of plumage, a truce was reached and, apart from the odd squabble, life on the pond is, once again, peaceful. I'm pleased to be able to tell you that, to date, I have counted, at one time, seven mandarins and two mallards on this tiny pond – it's amazing what a few handfuls of barley, scattered each day, can encourage.

I remember telling you, last August, about the pair of swallows that had been investigating my stables as a prospective nesting site --- well they're back, and if it's not the same pair, then I'll be very surprised. They were first noticed, a day or two ago, wheeling and twittering excitedly in the airspace above the paddocks. They quickly made repeated investigations of the interior of the stables and I sincerely hope that they'll take up residence; of course that's only if Isaac will let them. Isaac is a diminutive mule of unpredictable temperament who is currently occupying one of my boxes. He's tolerant of humans but has a hatred of cats and dogs and will chase both from the yard, or fields, if either should have the temerity to enter his space. All joking aside, I don't suppose for one minute that his presence will deter the swallows from nesting; indeed, they seem to prefer to share a location with animals and people, even if they are irritable and stubborn!

Must go for a 'swallow' myself.

July

The half term holiday has been and gone – thank goodness -- and, in the aftermath, a definite sense of peace and quiet has settled over the Inclosure. During this break from school thousands of visitors must have flocked to the Forest; many of whom could be seen red-faced and flustered as they peddled (or more often pushed) their unfamiliar hire-bikes up the steep gravelled rides in the baking sunshine. Frequently, their shouts, shrieks and vociferous admonitions to both wayward off-spring and defiant dogs echoed through the trees. But now we have a little respite and the ensuing silence allows the distant mewing of a pair of buzzards, who are, as I write, wheeling on outstretched wings, high in a clear, blue sky, to penetrate the inner sanctum of my study.

There's no doubt in my mind that the influx of our summer visitors causes considerable trauma to some of the inhabitants of the Forest and the absence of deer around the house and in the proximity of the cycle routes is indicative of this time of the year. Within the boundary of my lone property, however, the increased activity in the outside world is of little or no consequence to those who share my home with me. The ducks are not so frequent in their visits now although the mallard drake can be seen on most days. I guess that Mrs. Mallard and the tree-dwelling mandarins are either sitting on eggs or busy herding and protecting their ducklings; I often wonder if, in the fullness of time, we'll see their offspring or at least those that manage to escape the many hazards that they'll have to encounter before they are able to fly. Some birds have, once again, chosen to nest within the confines of the garden and paddocks and they include a pair of robins who have brazenly built in the bottom of the horses' feed bin in one of the lose boxes; Great tits are in the nest box on the wall above my study window and just around the corner, in the ivy, a pair of pied wagtails have already successfully reared and said farewell to their first brood. Enterprising wrens are safely ensconced in the centre of a dense palm tree and have probably chosen the most predator-free nesting site on the property, provided, of course, that Jack the Jack Russell keeps the grey squirrels at bay!!

The swallows have, after much dithering, taken a long time to construct their nest in the stable and, whilst I'm delighted to see these new-comers, I'm not sure that they're going to successfully produce a brood. They seem to be very erratic; they often disappear for two or three days and just when I give up all hope of their returning, they are suddenly there, swooping and twittering excitedly around the stable door and acting as though they had never been away. Whilst they were visiting the swallow equivalent of Tesco this morning I carried-out a little investigation and a mirror on a stick revealed two eggs in the cup-shaped nest which does make me more optimistic and I hope they continue to lay and hatch some chicks in the not too distant future. They don't seem at all concerned by their room-mate Isaac the mule but are very unsure about a human presence and I must say that I don't find this preference very flattering!

Sadly, there's still no sign of the flycatchers nor have I seen the colourful grey wagtails that have nested here for years. I'm sure it's too late now for either to make an appearance but I live in hope that next year might be different.

Once again the frogs have fooled me. My pond is not huge and despite close examination since early Spring I've seen no evidence of any frogspawn. Imagine my surprise and delight when, as I was feeding the ducks a few days ago, I noticed hundreds of wriggling 'Taddies' around the margins of the pond. I've no doubt that the ducks, grass snakes and others will account for many of them but some will survive to return in a few year time to lay their spawn.

Moving out of the Inclosure for a brief moment, I know that many of you will be interested to know, that whilst fishing in the Test valley recently with two like-minded colleagues, we observed, in less than two hours, a buzzard, a peregrine falcon, a sparrowhawk, a kestrel and last but by no means least an Osprey! What a privilege it was to see five of our native raptors in such a short time.

I must go now before I get in raptures over these raptors!!

August

After a long, hot spell we've had, at last, a few days of sensible rain and both the garden and the Forest seem to have come to life overnight. The rain sodden branches of the oak and beech have drooped under their new-found burden and revealed the embryonic promise of a good, autumnal harvest of acorns and mast which, in turn, will encourage the grey hordes of wood pigeons to descend on the Forest, as they have done in previous years. Similarly, hazel nuts are well advanced and the apple and blackberry crops look very promising. In the kitchen garden the rain has revitalised flagging plants and everything is standing upright and to attention except for, that is, my two rows of peas which have toppled over under the thrashing from the recent downpours. Never mind, a few canes will put them right and the skinny pods will soon fatten now they've had a good drenching. By the way, talking of peas, I have to say that I've never before had any success, up here, with this crop. Once sown, the seedling peas have always been devoured by the local mouse population -- until this year, that is, when I have a crop that would give Birdseye cause for concern -- and the secret? I'll tell you. I took some advice from an old and wise gardener and soaked the peas overnight in paraffin; another equally old but perhaps not so wise gardener pooh-poohed the idea and told me they'd never germinate. How wrong he was, the results speak for themselves and the Mice? Well they won't starve but I do seem to have lost a bottle of mouthwash!

Many of you kind people have asked after the well-being of my new cohabiters -- the swallows. In the July edition I reported that Mrs Swallow had layed two eggs and these were very soon joined by two more which eventually hatched into four chicks. Then, one day soon after their arrival, my mirror on a stick revealed only two remaining chicks. I searched the bare concrete floor below the nest and could find no sign of the missing birds so it seems that their demise will remain a mystery. Unlike the wagtails and blackbirds who have broods close by and who slave from dawn to dusk with beakfulls of food for the gaping maws of their offspring, my two swallows seem to spend most of the day at the beach; for hours they are nowhere to be seen and then suddenly they reappear and flit around with no apparent urgency to visit their young and scolding anyone who might be in the vicinity of their stable. Despite their seemingly negligent parents the two chicks are growing rapidly and appear to be contentedly replete and sleepy whenever I look in, I hope they make it.

The great spotted woodpeckers have had a successful breeding season and by the numbers visiting the nut feeders several broods have been hatched in the surrounding woodland. A few days ago I witnessed from my study window four young woodpeckers and one parent bird on or around one cage of peanuts. It was a delight to watch the fraught parent as it tried to wrestle food through the wire to feed its clamouring entourage. These young wood peckers are aggressive hooligans and with their bright red, punk haircuts they wreak havoc on the other residents in the garden and will readily chase off any one who dares to investigate one of their feeders, but they are a delight to watch.

We had some excitement here last night. A very presentable young man risked life and limb by coming unannounced through my front gate. My dogs were not impressed by his sudden intrusion and it took some persuasion from me to get them to settle. When he eventually managed to get a word in he explained that he was a London based school teacher who was looking for six girls who had failed to arrive at the final rendezvous of a Duke of Edinburgh navigation course. Fortunately they did have a mobile phone and had been able to tell him, with the aid of their map, that they were not far from my house and so he had come to find them. He rang them once again in my presence and after directing several questions to them we were able to establish that they were within sight of the A 31 and that they were on a 'white gravel track with grass growing on it'. I decided that this might be Sandy Ridge so with final instructions from their teacher to put on their hats and coats to keep warm we set-off in the Land Rover and drove through the fading light in, hopefully, the right direction. No, they weren't on Sandy Ridge but as I sat close to the A31 with the teacher next to me trying, once again, to make phone contact it suddenly occurred to me that their previous description of their location would also fit the redundant track behind Old House. So off we went and there in the middle of the track with a mist starting to fall were the six relieved young ladies. It was a tight squeeze to fit them all in the rear of the Land Rover but they were finally dropped back to their waiting minibus and their relieved school chums. Thank goodness they were equipped with a mobile phone.

Finally, my mushroom mentor has beaten me to it again and has already collected some tasty Chanterelles. This warm and moist weather will make many different species pop-up so with the mushroom pickers' code in mind take up your baskets and go hunting.

I like my mushrooming companion, in fact he's a fungus but there's not mushroom in this Forest for both of us!

Juvenile Male Great Spotted Woodpecker

September

No, I didn't really mean to call one of my best friends a Fungus! But those of you who read the end of the August piece of 'From the Inclosure' might well have noticed that, in fact, it would appear that I did. What you should have read was the word 'Fungi' i.e. a fun guy – get it? Unfortunately in this day and age of spell and grammar checkers somewhere in the ether between my PC and your copy of the magazine a grammatical correction was made -- and a perfectly correct alteration it was too; for the plural of fungus is fungi and as I was referring to a third person singular i.e. 'He' it was only right and proper that somewhere in cyber space an electronic brain chose to change my 'fungi' to 'fungus'. Whilst it made nonsense of my feeble attempt at word-play humour it did, at the same time, make a lot of us chuckle. I am sorry, my old friend, I'm sure that you weren't offended and you've probably chuckled more than the rest of us.

The swallows eventually managed to rear two chicks who took their first tenuous flight around the interior of the stables before finally zipping through the doors to explore the vastness of the open sky which was to be their domain for the rest of their days; or so I thought as I watched them flitting and twittering excitedly in the air-space above the paddocks, but little did I know that fate was about to deal a cruel hand. The next day I was wandering down to the stables to give Isaac the mule his morning toast when I noticed three swallows swooping and diving around the stable door, they seemed to be very agitated and were shouting loudly to each other. I knew that something was wrong but I wasn't prepared for what I saw when I looked over the door. There, hanging from the nest and quite dead, was one of the swallow chicks, I couldn't believe my eyes and was saddened to see its unfortunate demise. Closer inspection from a step -ladder revealed that a length of horse hair that had been used in the construction of the nest had somehow entangled in the feathers of one of its wing tips and the hapless little bird must have tried, unsuccessfully, to take flight and then hung, for goodness knows how long, before it finally gave up the struggle and died. Needless to say I removed it immediately and without further ado the remaining swallows disappeared and were not seen again until a few days ago when they suddenly reappeared as if by magic. This morning a bird swooped past my head as I walked by the door and on a sudden impulse I picked up my mirror which revealed, much to my surprise, four more pink-blotched eggs. I don't know how successful they will be in rearing a second brood this late in the season but I wish them better luck than they had with their first.

I took the dogs along the brook this morning and what a sorry sight it was for the river is virtually non-existent apart from isolated, semi-stagnant pools which must be providing a last-ditch sanctuary for those fish that haven't already succumbed to the devastating effects of low oxygen levels or the predations of both heron and mink. We wandered to the point by the gravel track where two streams merge to form Blackensford brook; the one known as Bartley Water rises in the bogs opposite the deer sanctuary and this was completely dry, the other, which springs from the mire in Backly Bottom and flows via Stinking Edge wood and Blackensford Lawn to join Bratley Water was producing no more than a feeble trickle. We are certainly desperately in need of a good drop of rain and the consequences of this on-going drought are beginning to become evident. Recently, especially at night when all is quiet, the silence has been suddenly broken by the ear-splitting rifle-crack and crashing thud as a large limb breaks from a thirsty tree. Whilst down by the bridge the ground beneath the hazel trees is littered with part formed nuts which have knuckled-off in the heat and in the lower reaches of the Lymington and Beaulieu rivers the sea trout are gathering and already changing colour as the unusually low water levels hinder their instinctive urge to travel up into the Forest streams to spawn.

My apple trees are suffering too and Isaac is getting a good supply of immature apples as they drop onto the grass below; but, on the other hand, the blackberries seem to revel in the hot sun and have produced an early, bumper crop. Now blackberry and apple is, in my opinion, a combination that can only have been made in Heaven so I've decided to freeze the blackberries until the apples have matured.

I'd better go, all this talk of blackberry and apple is giving me the pip!

October

The long drought continues and the unexpected downpour that we had during the night has done little or nothing to ease the plight of the gasping vegetables in the kitchen garden. There are signs, however, that a change in the seasons is imminent and, as I write, I can see, through my study widow, three fallow bucks who are industriously hoovering-up the amazingly plump acorns that have fallen onto the lawn below the oak trees. It is an idyllic sight and they are perfectly relaxed in each others company -- but not for long. During the next few weeks, as their testosterone levels increase, their neck muscles will thicken and their Adams Apples will become very prominent and soon it will be each man for himself as the rutting season begins. Mature bucks will establish rutting stands where they will thrash trees and wallow in the mud (if we get some rain!) and pace up and down groaning and belching in a manner that is intended to attract their does. These rutting stands are fiercely guarded and some epic battles will take place between the resident buck and any interloper who should dare to look twice at his females. Even now, in the quiet of the night, I can hear the 'clack', 'clack' of antlers as some of the bucks spar with each other in anticipation of the battles to come. If you should care to take a walk through the enclosure during the month of October then you may well hear their groaning calls or the rattling clash of feuding antlers.

I'm sure that some of you must be getting fed-up with the on-going saga of my new lodgers, the swallows, and if you are, then I apologise for going on about them and this will be the last mention, this year. The four eggs in the second clutch that I talked about last month hatched far quicker than the first brood and the young birds developed at an alarming pace. The rattle of the stable door would cause four yellow, gaping beaks to appear over the rim of the nest and the adult birds were around the yard continuously as they strived to satisfy the hunger of their ever growing chicks. Everything seemed to be going well for these charming little birds until, that is, a few days ago, when fate dealt another cruel blow. I had gone down to check on Isaac the mule and as soon as I'd reached the stable yard I was aware of an ominous silence. Gone were the warning twitters that the swallows used each time I approached their nest site and the constant coming and going of the industrious birds was noticeable by its absence. I scanned the sky hoping to see the blue and white arrows streaking toward the stables – but there was no sign of them. I looked over the stable door and rattled the catch. There was no response from the swallow chicks and then I noticed, on the concrete floor below the nest, a dead fledgling. I picked it up and it was quite cold it had been dead for some time and then, with the aid of my mirror, I looked in the nest and discovered that the other three fledglings were also dead. I was saddened by their demise and can only assume that one or both of the parent birds had been killed and as a result, the hapless chicks had starved to death. It's been a good year for sighting hobbies in this part of the Forest and these small, swift-shaped raptors are particularly fond of swallows and martins so there's a good chance that one of these beautifully designed hunters could have been the swallows' downfall.

On a much lighter note and following the excellent article on nightjars by Andrew Norris, which was printed in the August edition, I was delighted to receive a call from a good friend who had come across the nest of a pair of these strange and mysterious birds.

Nightjar Chicks

He invited me to photograph the chicks and later that evening I met him at the appointed spot and followed him across the heather on an open area of the Forest. Nightjars usually nest in clear-felled areas where they are able to blend invisibly with the background so I was a little puzzled by our location but before I had time to air my thoughts and within three-hundred yards of the car park an adult nightjar flapped from the heather in front of us and began to trail a wing, just like a lapwing, when you get too close to its nest. Cautiously, we crept up to the nest site and there, in nothing more than a scrape in the dried plant litter, were two of the ugliest little birds imaginable. I quickly took some photos and marvelled at how well they blended into their surroundings and then without further delay we backed-off some distance and watched as the parent bird returned to its charges. It was a rare and privileged sighting and, thanks to a thoughtful friend, one that I'll never forget.

This month I've also been able to add another species to my list of birds that have been seen over or in my property. I was sitting on the patio having a cup of tea with a like-minded friend when we heard a 'Kronk'. We both looked up and said, simultaneously, "Raven" and there, flying over the paddock, was the largest member of the crow family.

Look out for them, they're making quite a come-back on the Forest and they're easily identified by their sheer size, their kronking call and their long necks.

I must finish now, before you think I've gone raven mad

November

It's early October and the drought is well and truly over. The streams and rivers are flowing freely and it's not difficult to imagine the sea trout, in the lower reaches of the Beaulieu and the Lymington rivers who, sensing the increased flows are preparing themselves, at long last, for their final journey high into the Forest streams where they will spawn in the gravel beds. Bogs and winter-born ponds that have been bone-dry are now beginning to fill and Wellie-boots are the order of the day when walking in some of the low-lying parts of the Forest. Despite the heavy rain the temperatures remain high and the effect of this combination is, like the curates egg, good in parts. In the garden the grass is growing at an Amazonian rate and as it's constantly saturated by either the regular downpours or the ground-soaking dews the best I can do is to trim the top in between showers and similarly, the weeds in the paths, borders and kitchen garden are growing so fast that I don't quite know where to start. On the Forest, however, the humid weather has encouraged the best season, that I can remember, for one of the most delicious and much sought after mushrooms. Boletus edulis know as the penny bun in England, cep in France and porcini in Italy is, without doubt, a prince among fungi. Look for it along the edges of Forest plantations particularly near beech trees; sometimes they will be found growing close to the fly agaric fungus and this can be a good marker for their location for the fly agaric is the bright scarlet, white-flecked toadstool that some of us will remember in the illustrations of our childhood story books. Despite its aesthetic appearance and its nostalgic associations it is poisonous and should never be eaten; it does however have very strong associations with the origins of Father Christmas and his flying reindeer but more about this in the December edition.

The humid weather has also produced a plethora of field mushrooms and these tasty, white fungi can be seen winking in the cropped grass of paddocks and along road-side, Forest verges. The more observant or experienced may have found, already, a picking or two of the golden, egg-yolk, yellow chanterelles; but be careful it's also a very good year for the false chanterelles and the inexperienced could easily confuse these for the real thing and, trust me, you really don't want to eat these by mistake! Just remember, if you do go out to gather fungi, only pick those mushrooms that you can recognise, without any doubt, as being edible. Don't put unknown fungi in your basket with mushrooms you are going to eat; the spores from the unknown species may contaminate your good fungi and could make you very sick – or worse! It is recommended that no more than 1.5kg are collected per visit so please do not over pick; fungi forays are getting increasingly popular and it's essential that we ensure a supply for the future.

Have you noticed the size of the chestnuts this year? They're enormous and well worth gathering if you can get to them before the deer and the ponies, that is. It's a wonder that we're having such a bumper Forest harvest after such a prolonged period of drought, but I suppose that conditions earlier in the year were just right when the flowers were formed and the insects and other creatures were in abundance to assist with the pollination and ensure the future of the species.

There have been some clear nights recently and the Harvest moon has been a sight to behold but the temperature has dropped quite dramatically on several occasions and most mornings after one of these cold snaps I've

Raft Spider

been greeted by the sight of large spiders in the either the bath or the Belfast sink. I've no doubt that they enter the house at this time of year in search of somewhere warmer and whilst they don't bother me, I know that some of you ladies would prefer that they remained outside! Whilst we're talking about spiders, next time you venture onto the Forest and happen upon a pond, look closely for a large, handsome, russet-brown spider with a creamy-white stripe either side of its abdomen. You'll probably spot one of these if you stand quietly and watch among the water vegetation. This is the raft spider (Dolomedes fimbriatus) and it just loves the acidic ponds of the New Forest. The raft spider (and no it doesn't build a raft) has fine hairs on the tips of its legs which enable it to walk across any still, water surface. It feeds on all kinds of aquatic life such as pond skaters and damsel flies and will even take tadpoles and small fish. It hunts by sitting on some convenient waterside vegetation with its two front legs, which act as sensors, resting on the water surface and then, when it feels the vibration of nearby prey, it dashes across the water to secure its meal.

More information about spiders can be found on the Web!!

December

Halloween and Bonfire night are now in the past, as far as 2006 is concerned and now Christmas and the festive season hurtle towards us and one only has to open a newspaper or switch on the television to realise what an enormously commercial venture it has become. But where did it all begin? Well, we're all aware that on 25th December we celebrate the birth of the baby Jesus but there are many other strange and unrelated rituals and myths that surround this time of the year, not least of whom are Father Christmas and his flying reindeer.

So where has this jolly man with his red cheeks and equally red suit, which traditionally is fastened with white buttons, come from? There's a very plausible and fascinating explanation which is rooted in the Fly Agaric mushroom that I mentioned briefly in last months edition. The Fly Agaric (Amanita muscaria) is the stunning bright-scarlet, white-spotted fungus that will be familiar to most people who either live or walk in the Forest, whilst others may well remember it as the fairy-tale toadstool in the story book illustrations of their childhood. But beware, for despite its aesthetic appearance and its romantic associations this fungus is poisonous and should never, under any circumstances, be eaten. It does, in fact, contain powerful hallucinogenic toxins and anyone who is stupid enough to eat it will become violently sick. It derives its name from a practice which dates back to medieval times when pieces of the mushroom were placed into a bowl of milk in order to stupefy and kill any flies that came to drink from it.

Fly Agaric is common throughout most of the Northern hemisphere and is much loved by many species of deer but especially by reindeer who readily consume it despite its alarming effects. Now, apparently, Rudolph the red-nosed reindeer has a very shiny nose and so it would seem, if we are to believe the many pictures of him on seasonal cards and wrapping paper, does Father Christmas. These colourful appendages could well be the result of the consumption of this highly inebriant toadstool which has been and still is held in high regard by some cultures. Indeed, in remote parts of north-eastern Siberia live the Koryak people who are shamanistic, nomadic, reindeer herders for whom the Fly Agaric is a major influence in their rituals and beliefs, which are so similar to our own myth of Father

Christmas and his flying reindeer that they cannot be discounted as a likely origin.

Fly Agaric (Amanita muscaria)

An ingestion of the toxins contained in this fungus will create the hallucination of flight and will also cause objects to appear larger than they actually are; in fact it's said that this was the mushroom that Alice consumed in Lewis Carrolls' Through the Looking Glass, the effects of which, if you remember, made the door appear larger and thus enabled Alice to slip underneath. Now, having watched their reindeer consume a good quantity of this colourful dish the Koryak were impressed by the phenomenal leaps made by their beasts in their exaggerated attempts to jump over ridiculously small objects. This ability to 'fly' together with the reindeers' capacity to trek for excessively long periods without sleep would have made them the perfect choice of all the animals to haul Santas' sleigh – don't you think?

But where does Father Christmas come into this? Well, the Koryak, who weren't slow to notice that after a fungi-feast their reindeer seemed to be possessed of amazing powers and were devoid of fear, decided to have a go at the Fly Agaric themselves. As I told you earlier, the ingestion of Fly

Agaric results in violent sickness and no doubt, after many unsuccessful and unfortunate experiments, they finally discovered that the safest way to minimise this debilitating reaction was to process them in some way, so they were usually dried, made into a drink, or smoked.   There were some rituals, however, where the Shaman or Medicine Man was called upon to play a major role which started with a period of four or five days during which he fasted. He then consumed, on an empty stomach, a good quantity of this poisonous mushroom which of course made him terribly ill and violently sick; you are probably, like me, beginning to think that being the Shaman was not the best job in the world and perhaps suited to the more gullible members of society! But it doesn't end there, once the sickness has passed his eager followers collected and drank his urine, (which after the fasting was mainly water together with the dissolved toxins from the fungus), so that they too could partake of its hallucinogenic effects without having to be subjected to the same violent reactions that the daft Shaman had just been through. So, it would seem that the Fly Agaric was an important and essential part of Koryak culture and much revered by these nomads; it inhibited fear and the startle reflex and apparently left a feeling of well being after the effects of the drug had worn off, unless of course you happened to be the Shaman!

The Koryak are a nomadic people who live, during the summer months, in yurts which are portable, rounded tents but during the winter period they construct a more substantial dwelling and, because of the extreme build-up of snow at this time of the year, access to the interior can only be made through a hole in the roof which also acts as a smoke hole for the fire. During midwinter festivals the Shaman, no doubt flushed and feeling very much under the weather, arrives by reindeer sleigh and bearing a sack containing dried Fly Agaric, as gifts for the household, he enters each dwelling via the smoke hole (is this beginning to sound familiar?) and after conducting his ceremony and no doubt taking some refreshment he takes his leave by the same route.

Our own Father Christmas is dressed in a red suit with white buttons which is said to symbolise the Fly Agaric. He travels from his home in the frozen North in a sleigh pulled by flying reindeer and carries a sack filled with special gifts and he enters and leaves our homes via the chimney. So what do you think, have Santa and Rudolph been derived from the Koryak Shaman and his reindeer? They might be!

Have a good Christmas and watch what you eat!

January

2006 was quite a year and we suffered one of the toughest and most prolonged droughts on record; searching back through my scribblings I noticed that I mentioned the dire state of the river below the house during the months of August and September but, if you could've seen it recently, you would've found it hard to imagine that it was, not so long ago, nothing more than a dried-up channel with occasional, isolated, semi-stagnant pools. I'd been told by an excited friend that the sea trout were, at last, running up the section of the stream that had been reshaped in 2005and 2006 as part of the LIFE 3 project so, without delay, off I set with the dogs to investigate this annual event. As I walked down the hill to the river I could see that the water had breached the banks in many places and I could hear, long before I reached the bottom of the valley, the gurgling and gulping of the swollen torrent as it plunged recklessly towards the sea. Suddenly, I noticed a flash of white in the downstream trees and thought at once that it was the white fallow buck that had been hanging around the house in recent days; but I was wrong, closer inspection revealed it to be a wall of foam that had been whipped-up by the angry waters on one of the sharper bends in the river, but it looked very lifelike as it bobbed and bounced on the boiling surface. There was no way that I would be able to spot any fish in that turmoil so after giving the dogs a chance to stretch their legs we, reluctantly, headed home.

The following day I decide to return to the river in the hope that things might have calmed down and, to my amazement, the only sign of the floodwaters were the occasional pools on the forest floor that had been left by the receding river. A fairly tranquil stream chattered past me and the watery sunlight glinted on patches of golden, fresh-washed gravel in the river bed in which the exhausted sea trout will deposit their eggs before beginning their long and arduous journey back to the sea. I began to wander along the bank and, to my delight, I hadn't gone far when a ripple in the water surface told me that a sea trout had just moved hastily off a shallow, gravel redd (which is the name given to the gravel in which a sea trout spawns) and darted into the sanctuary of a deeper, upstream pool. I proceeded now with greater care and over the next hour or so was rewarded by several sightings of these truly remarkable and tenacious fish.

I was delighted by the outcome of my little excursion and decided to cut across the Forest on my homeward journey. I whistled for the dogs to follow and noticed that my geriatric cocker, who still has a marvellous nose but whose eyesight and hearing leave much to be desired, was deeply engrossed in something under a clump of spindly trees. I was about to retrace my steps in order to get her attention when, with a waggle of her stubby tail, she flushed a pair of woodcock that jinked silently away through the trees. These were, almost certainly, the harbingers of many more who will soon arrive from colder climes to over-winter with us – and jolly glad I was, to see them.

Not long after the woodcock sighting I climbed up into Bratley wood and I had gone no more than a few steps into the shadows of the ancient trees when the noise from the wings of hundreds of pigeons assailed my ears as a blue-grey cloud rose from the Forest floor and made a getaway through the almost leafless branches. These too had migrated from colder areas and had descended on the Forest to gorge on the bumper harvest of beech mast and acorns and I was even more delighted by their arrival.

I returned home a happy and contented man and as I dozed off that night I was running the wonderful sightings of the day through my sleepy mind. It seemed that I had just succumbed to sleep when I was rudely awoken by barking dogs and as I struggled to find the light switch I was surprised to see that it was, in fact, 3 o'clock in the morning. I staggered out of bed and switched on the powerful security lights and immediately I could see, through my study window, the source of the problem for there, on the edge of the beam, was the ghostly outline of a grey pony and as I stared into the night I became aware of other, darker forms around her. Like the pigeons these ponies, oblivious to the disturbance they had caused, were hoovering-up the acorns from beneath a large oak tree. The dogs refused to settle until I had allowed them to investigate, for themselves, the strange noises that had caused them to wake me and, after the house had settled down, I eventually returned to my slumber. I don't know why I did but, before I crept into bed, I lifted the blind and looked out onto the brightly illuminated patio and there, despite all the noise and disturbance, perched on the back of a garden chair was a beautiful tawny owl. I rushed for the camera but before I could open the window sufficiently to allow for a snap it suddenly launched into the air and glided away on silent wings. What a marvellous way to end a day full of lovely surprises.   Have a marvellous new year

March

Yesterday, I cut my lawn for the first time this year. Not exactly earth-shattering news, I know, but in past years the first cut has not been necessary until later on into the spring and at this time of the year the ground is usually far too soft for the ride-on mower. The mild winter that we've had so far has meant that the grass didn't stop growing, it just slowed up and the unseasonably dry spell that we've had for the past few days has dried and firmed the rain-soaked ground. But the grass is not the only thing that has continued to grow unchecked, the ivy on the walls of the house is invading the roof and I'll have to get the ladder out before it gets out of control! I've also noticed several people cutting hedges in and around the village and it's a good thing to get the first trim of the year over and done with before the birds start nesting in earnest. However, by the time you read this in March some of the early hedge-nesting birds might well have completed their construction projects so it's a good idea, if you have to trim a hedge, to wander slowly along its length to see if you can identify any new nests. If it's at all possible to look up through the foliage from below then do so, nests are so much easier to spot in this way.

When you have completed the operation please, please, please clear the cuttings and dispose of them in such a way that the commoners livestock can't get at them. I've been asked to mention this by a concerned commoner who has suffered losses in the past when his beasts have been poisoned by eating hedge trimmings that have been left in the road or dumped onto the Forest

If you do happen to cut close to an active nest don't be too distressed; most birds can be quite reluctant to move when disturbed and if left alone will, more than likely, continue about their business. Several years ago, whilst cutting an extremely overgrown and rampant cotoneaster, I unwittingly cut off the clump of twiglets that a pair of spotted fly catchers had chosen as a nest site; and what's more, the nest contained four, tiny blue-green eggs. I was upset by what I had done and I carefully placed the bundle of twigs and nest into a cleft in a nearby azalea. Ten minutes or so later I stopped for a break and was surprised to see the fly catchers flitting agitatedly around their former home. Carefully, I gathered up the nest and placed it, as near as I could remember, into the now shorn site of

39

its former location and I built a little bower of leaves over it to provide shade from the sun.   I was delighted to observe the return of the fly catchers and in a few days, after the eggs had hatched, the male bird was kept extremely busy by catching and carrying huge numbers of flies back to his brooding mate.   Sadly this story doesn't have a happy ending, just as the chicks were almost fully fledged, I noticed both parent birds behaving oddly around the nest site and before I could do anything to prevent it a magpie swooped down from the roof of the barn and snatched the remaining chick.   It had already devoured the others without my knowing.

Sometimes life just isn't fair

Robin

April

Thank goodness I did cut my grass when I had the opportunity because conditions since then have definitely prevented further gardening activity of any description. In fact it's so wet up here that the runner bean seeds, the onion sets and the shallots are sitting in the garden shed patiently awaiting a dry spell which will enable me to plant them – something that should have been done long before now! But not to worry, Mother Nature has a way of balancing her accounts and I'm sure that everything will get planted in time and nothing will suffer unduly because of any delay in our traditional sowing times.

After a particularly frightful night, when the howling wind came down the chimney and blew wood ash into the room whilst the rain lashed noisily against the windows, we have awoken to a beautiful spring day. Once again the early morning forest is alive with the dawn chorus as the cock birds of many species do their damnedest to convince the ladies of the parish that they are the best of the bunch. Great spotted woodpeckers can be heard drumming on their trees as they convey to all and sundry that this is their patch of Forest and in the background wood pigeons have started their "Go Back Betty" calls.

As I sit in my eyrie writing I can see, in the grass ride that runs out to the main gravel track, a pair of crows who are busily turning over the leaf-litter in search of some tasty morsels. They appear very relaxed and why shouldn't they be? Carrion crows mate for life, so they don't have to endure the frantic fighting and courtship displays that are very much a way of life, at springtime, for most of the other birds. They weren't quite so relaxed earlier this morning, however, when their largest cousin, a raven, chose to make a fly-past. In fact, it was only the racket they were making in their attempts to drive it away that encouraged me to stir from my desk to investigate. Sadly, after such a rude greeting, the raven didn't linger, but like the crows they don't stray far from their nesting site at this time of year; and whilst the crows probably won't lay any eggs until the end of March, the female raven will almost certainly be incubating her four to six eggs and our earlier visitor was more than likely her mate, who like the male crow, will feed his wife on the nest.

Grey squirrels have, suddenly, appeared like magic. A week or so ago they were rarely seen and now, just as if someone has thrown a light switch, the little varmints are everywhere. As the sun begins to slide away behind Woolfield Hill there are three on the Forest floor searching for the acorns that they buried last autumn and at the same time an energetic male is giving an elusive female a death-defying chase up the vertical trunk of the old oak tree and through its still naked branches.

Cock Pheasants Fighting

As I watch the antics of the squirrels a slight movement catches my eye and there, tentatively picking its way out of the cover, is a small deer with large ears. It's a roe deer and as it turns away from me I can see the 'tush' of hair which tells me it's a doe; for although the roe deer has no tail the female grows this tail-like tuft of hair which makes her easy to distinguish from an immature buck or a mature buck that has shed its antlers.

Off to see another buck now – a White one!

May

I slipped away for Easter. I left the Forest and took a flight from Southampton to Guernsey – only twenty five minutes flying time but what a difference that short distance can make. The weather was stunning; hot balmy days with bees and hover flies taking full advantage of the unseasonably warm weather and wild flowers in such profusion that every turn in the road or bend in a path revealed a stunning display of just about every species of spring bloom. The air was ladened with the heady perfume of the bluebells that clothed the steep sides of the water lanes and on the cliff tops, sea pinks and both red and white campions jostled for position. The digital camera was in constant use and I thanked those very clever people who invented it; I came home with 168 photographs but just think what the cost in film and processing might have been if I had taken the old 35mm camera!

My trip was short lived, just three days, but it was nice to get away for a break and equally pleasant to come home to Gods country, here in the Forest, and to see the changes that had occurred in such a short period of time. The oak, hawthorn and silver birch trees had opened their buds and pushed forth their tiny, new spring leaves and as I stood near the Canadian war memorial on Easter Monday and looked over Slufters Inclosure, a hint of green was showing in the previously bare canopy. Later in the day I strolled down the garden and the smell from the laurel, now in full flower, was a delight to the senses and similarly as I walked the dogs, in the evening, along the forest track the stately fir trees emitted their unmistakable smell of treacle sponge pudding.

But not everything is pleasant at this time of the year! I was relaxing with a book in the conservatory on the final evening of the holiday when I was attacked by the first of the spring midges and was forced to retreat to the inner sanctum of the sitting room. How I hate these miniscule pests whose bites bring me out in huge, irritating hives and why do they make a bee-line for me and leave others untouched? They really do spoil my spring and summer months but not nearly so much as the deer ticks which, once again, have been in evidence throughout our relatively mild winter. The dogs, of course, are prime targets and provide an eminently suitable host for these blood-sucking pests and checking their coats, for any unwanted guests, has now become part of our daily routine.

We had a minor emergency the other day when I returned, after a short shopping trip, to find my Jack Russell, in obvious distress with his left eye closed and weeping.

I examined the eye and where the lower lid joins the eyeball there was a foreign particle that refused to budge when I tried to remove it. Closer inspection revealed that it was a tick and the hideous creature was latched firmly to the poor little dogs' eye. I immediately phoned those lovely people at Mid-Forest Vets and they very kindly held the surgery open so that I could bring the patient in for treatment. A few drops of anesthetic in the eye and a deft hand with the tweezers swiftly resolved the problem. The little dog was none the worse for the experience, but think how painful it could have been if the repulsive thing had remained in there for any length of time!

I'd better go before I get a ticking-off for rambling on.

Bluebell Wood

June

What do you think about this weather? Here we are the spring bank holiday weekend and, apart from a few miserable drops, we haven't seen any rain for weeks. My Father, who's in his 91st year, has consistently, (on the basis that he's seen all this changing weather before in his lifetime), pooh-poohed the idea of global warming but he's had to admit that he can't remember an April like the one just gone!

Blackensford brook is beginning to look like it did in the height of the summer, last year; I walked along it just a few days ago and the little river is reduced to isolated pools which are linked by babbling shallows that can easily be forded without the aid of Wellington boots. Out on the Forest some of the wetland areas seem to be suffering too from the lack of precipitation and it's possible, at the moment, to walk across considerable tracts of bog that would normally be quite impassable at this time of the year.

It may be a time to consider the old proverb:

Oak before Ash, in for a splash
Ash before oak, in for a soak

Which is meant to say that if the oak buds open before the ash then we will be in for a dry summer, but if the ash buds open before the oak then we'll be in for a wet summer? Well let me tell you now, that up here in the Inclosure, the oak was in leaf long before any ash! So look out!

The unseasonably warm weather has not deterred the birds from doing what they normally do at this time of the year and I'm sharing my house, as usual, with several other families. Mum and Dad robin have chosen my back porch as a suitable location to rear their young which has meant that to avoid disturbing them, all traffic, into and out of the house, has been through the front kitchen door. Above my study window, in the pyrocanthus, is the nest of a pair of pied wagtails and immediately adjacent to it, their cousins, the grey wagtails, have also elected to build. In fact their nests are so close that they must disturb each others youngsters, every time they return with food.

Last week a pair of swallows appeared and without hesitation began to inspect the interior of Isaacs stable. I was delighted to see them of course and I hope they're the same pair, or offspring from the same pair, who tried so stoically, last year, to be the first ever of their species to nest on this site. Quite frankly, I hadn't expected to see any swallows this year and was amused when recently an enterprising wren decided to cap-off the swallows nest with a smart, moss lid and thus transformed it into a potential home where his mate might lay her eggs. The male wren builds several nests each spring and then invites his missus to select the one that takes her fancy and because I hadn't seen any wren activity around the stable I'd assumed that this particular nest had not been to her liking.

I decided to encourage the swallows to stay by removing, without delay, this unexpected extension to their home. You can imagine my surprise when, as I mounted the step ladder, an angry little ball of brown feathers flew out of the entrance hole and sat bobbing noisily on the top of the stable wall. Needless to say I left her alone – and the rightful owners?

They'll just have to swallow their pride and build again.

Swallows Nest Capped-off by a Wren

July

The British weather must be the most unpredictable subject to write about. Last month I was rattling on to you about the April drought and I'd no sooner sent my ramblings to the editor when, what do you think? Yes, the heavens opened and down came the rain; in fact as I sit here, writing, the rain is lashing against the window and the weather lady, on the radio, has just informed me that, in the past three days, we've had the equivalent, for this time of the year, of one months' rainfall. I don't doubt her either for I noted yesterday, in the time that it took me to walk the dogs out to the A31 and back again, that the water level in Blackensford brook rose by eighteen inches (that's 450 mm for the converted).

So, let's talk about something a little more reliable. Have you noticed the foxgloves this year? They are definitely finding the weather to their liking. Look out for them in areas of clear-felled forest where they will have clothed the bare Forest floor with a stunning display of colour. These tall plants are capable of bearing dozens of purple, finger shaped flowers. Hence their name Digitalis purpurea (Digitalis as in digit or finger and purpurea as in purple); whereas the common name of *foxglove* has nothing at all to do with foxes. It is in fact a derivation of 'folks' gloves for our forebears believed that fairy folk used to wear the flowers as gloves. It provides a marvellous food source for bees and is also the source of the drug Digitalis which, I believe, is used in the treatment of heart conditions

The swallows, for those of you who frequently ask after their wellbeing have, at last, built a new nest. It's immediately opposite their old abode which had been converted by the wrens to a more salubrious dwelling. The magic 'mirror on a stick' has revealed three, white eggs, each with reddish-brown speckles, nestling in the feather lining and I guess that the hen bird will probably lay a couple more before she starts to incubate her first brood. I say her first brood because I'm convinced that these swallows are novice parents since they took so long to build their nest and, quite frankly, it's a complete mess. Compared to the neat little nest which was constructed last summer by more experienced builders this one is a muddle of mud and grass, much of which hangs in long, untidy strands and I'm sure that, if there was such a thing as an avian building inspector, this structure would without doubt be condemned!

Many of you will be aware that some three years ago the fickle wind of fate gave us our first sighting of a rather rare pair from the east coast of America who suddenly appeared, with one young offspring, into our village. They soon found a suitable nest (despite some noisy neighbours) in the Beeches and having overcome some interesting and sometimes amusing language problems they proved to be extremely friendly and melded unobtrusively into our Forest ways and very quickly became an important part of our finely balanced ecosystem. Sadly the Big Apple is calling and the urge to return from

Young Ross Middleton

whence they came is upon them. This village will be a poorer place with their leaving so let's hope that they'll become 'cross- pond' migrants and that they'll return at least once a year to see us. So, to Glen, Joanne and Ross Middleton – our American friends - thank you for sharing some of your time with us. We'll all miss you.

Good luck and bon voyage

August

I'm feeling rather virtuous this morning. Whilst most of you were still in your beds I was up, not long after the sun, and with mushroom basket and dogs I was away across the Forest for a good walk - and not before time. The horrendous weather of late June and early July had meant that walking could only be considered if the feet were encased in hot Wellie boots and the body was swathed in equally sweltering waterproofs. Not this morning, however, shirt sleeves and light trousers were the order of the day and good, stout leather boots provided sufficient protection to keep the feet comfortable. The early morning sun was very welcome as it crept through my shirt to warm my back; the dogs, too, seemed to revel in the more seasonal conditions and with tails erect and noses down they trotted along the track in front of me with a new-found spring in their paws.

We reached the cross-roads in the track and turned towards the brook. The dogs stepped-up the pace as soon as they realised that we were heading for the river and I couldn't deny them the chance of a dip in the babbling water. It didn't seem possible that a few yards upstream and just a few days before we'd had a very unnerving experience; the water, unlike today, was brown and turbulent and swollen by the never-ending rains that threatened to burst its banks in several places. It swirled and formed eddies and whirlpools around the fallen trees and other debris and I was just thinking to myself that I wouldn't have much of a chance if I fell in, when there was aloud splash from behind. I turned and was horrified to see that my elderly cocker- Mad Lulu- had fallen, from a steep-sided bank, into the maelstrom below and I watched in despair as she was swept helplessly downstream. With failing eyesight and almost totally deaf the little dog looked totally bewildered as, helplessly, she was spun round and round by the relentless current. Ancient legs that had once retrieved a huge Canada goose across the mighty river Avon now trod uselessly against the force of the water and, hindered by layers of protective clothing, I struggled to keep pace with her as she was carried away. Benson, (yes, brother of Hedges) my black Lab knew that something was amiss and encouraged me in my pursuit by barking excitedly and running ahead. Fortunately, Lady Luck was with us on that day for just beyond a bend in the river there was Benson bouncing around on a raised shingle bank that had been washed down by the storms. I followed the dogs' example and jumped down onto the shelf just in time to pluck my geriatric pooch from the torrent as she swept past. With a quick shake and stagger she recovered her composure and, as though nothing had happened, she trotted off without a hint of a 'thank you'.

Dogs, I'm sure, are cannier than we give them credit for and as I was writing the previous paragraph I was distracted by the incessant barking of my Jack Russell and forced to leave my desk to go and investigate. I followed the tiresome noise and found him yapping away and dancing back and forth at something under the garden hedge. I had a good idea, before I looked, that I knew what was causing his concern.

Young Jack

I called the little dog away and with a 'where the hell've you been' look he reluctantly backed- off and there, curled-up in the leaf litter, was a beautiful, mature adder.

The reptile was quickly removed before it could do any damage and peace reigned once again in the Inclosure. But tell me, how did that dog who, true to breed, would normally chomp anything that moves, know that the adder was not to be trifled with?

Snakes alive! Is that the time – must go now

September

It doesn't seem possible that it's September once again; and what a year this has been, so far. Unseasonably hot weather in the early part of the year which was followed by the wettest summer since records began. We are all too aware of the plight of some of the unfortunate people, in places like Tewkesbury, where severe flooding has caused enormous damage to those properties that were foolishly built in the low-lying flood plains of our rivers. Spare a thought too for our long suffering farmers with marooned cattle to feed and hay and cereal crops lying sodden in inaccessible fields and who now live in abject fear of the dreaded Foot and Mouth disease that has suddenly, once again, reared its ugly head in our countryside.

The unusual weather patterns seem to have had a most unusual effect on some of our plants. The beech mast is ready to drop in some areas and the leaves of this most noble of trees are staring to turn; I just hope that the mast will be there, later in the year, when the animals need it- but it does seem rather early for it to be falling. In the kitchen garden both the runner beans and the broad beans have been a disaster with only a single picking off each! Sweet peas, that last year were a wall of colour, are stunted and there's not a single bloom to be seen but I live in hope that there may still be time for them to produce a few flowers. On the up-side I have been picking Purple Sprouting Broccoli which, as the gardeners among you will know, is usually grown as a useful vegetable for harvesting in that lean period between late winter and early spring and, don't ask me why but for the first time ever, I've been picking delicious, fat, ripe figs from the little potted tree on the patio. Out in the Forest we have been blessed with a plethora of the lovely, egg-yolk yellow Chanterelle mushrooms as well as a few early Ceps together with some ridiculously early Hedgehog mushrooms and the sinister looking but delicious Horn of Plenty or as our French cousins call them Trompettes des Morts.

Whilst we are on the subject of edible Fungi some of you have asked me how to distinguish between the true Chanterelle (Cantharellus cibarius) and the False Chanterelle (Hygrophoropsis aurantiaca), so here we go. The Chanterelle or Girolle, as it is sometimes called, starts life as a small flat cap with a down-curved edge and rapidly develops into a large funnel-shaped mushroom up to 10 cm across with a wavy and irregular margin.

The stunning colour of the Chanterelle is also likened to apricots and, surprise, surprise; it has the faint fragrant smell of apricots too.

Egg-yolk, Yellow Chanterelle

Look for this excellent specimen in the moss and leaf litter under the canopy of oak and beech woods and occasionally under coniferous trees. The False Chanterelle, which bears a slight resemblance to the real thing, grows predominately in coniferous forests and on heathland, it remains only shallowly funnel-shaped and is orange-yellow in colour with a strong, mushroomy smell. The gills on the underside of the Girolle are randomly forked whilst those of the False Chanterelle branch only into two. In truth, if you saw both species together you would have no hesitation in distinguishing the edible specimen but please remember, if you have the slightest doubt about the identity of a mushroom then leave it alone; don't touch it, don't pick it and certainly don't eat it.

Must go now- there's not mushroom to write any more!

October

Have you seen the heather this year? I don't know what it's like now but, at the time of writing, it's absolutely stunning. Perhaps, if you didn't notice the luxuriant, purple cloak that the Forest was wearing, you may have been aware, as you travelled about your business, of the delicious smell of honey that pervaded the air – this was, of course, the smell of the heather and, having spoken to some who are older and wiser than me, it would seem that this year could well be the best heather year in living memory.

Yesterday, I came upon an elderly gentleman perched upon a folding stool close to the Canadian War Memorial. I bade him a good morning and he assured me that it most certainly was and went on to ask if I could account for the pleasant smell that was being carried towards us on the light, north –westerly breeze. I explained that it was the heather and, immediately, I could see that he was not entirely happy with my response. He went on to say that he had been coming to the Forest for many years but could not remember smelling the heather before now – I assured him that he was not alone and that several people had told me just the same. Similarly, a friend of mine had occasion to fly over the Forest after taking off from Southampton airport and she tells me that the view from the air was simply breathtaking and so striking that it encouraged other passengers to comment on the sight. The dogs, now unfettered by the earlier restrictions that were imposed on them to protect the ground nesting birds, kick up purple puffs of heather pollen as they charge through the wiry shrubs. Whilst, out on the open Forest, beehives stand in rows like distant tower blocks – taller this year than normal because of the glut of honey from the heather which has necessitated the addition of extra frames. I can't wait to get my hands on some of the final product!

The August bank holiday is now just a memory and with the start of the school term the pressure on the Forest is somewhat relieved. Fallow and roe deer are seen more frequently around the cottage now that the numbers of visitors have diminished and the dogs bark less frequently at lost tourists who hover around the gate in the hope that someone from within will come to their aid. On the outside Forest lawn grey squirrels are, in anticipation of the coming winter, busily stowing food into secret caches – so secret that they probably won't find them when they need them!

Heather near Canada Cross

Meanwhile, in the stable, all is quiet. The swallows successfully reared a second brood of chicks this year and although they departed their nest in early September I'm sure the mild weather and the bounteous supply of food will help them on their long journey to warmer climes.

But all around us are the signs that the Forest and its inhabitants are slowly shutting down in preparation for the long nights and short days of winter. The fallow rut will be upon us before we know it and with a bit of luck and, dare I say it, a drop of rain, we will still have plenty of time to gather a few mushrooms for the store cupboard. The trees are starting to turn and the Forest will once again become a blaze of autumn colours and just think how we will all enjoy clearing all those lovely leaves that will soon be covering our lawns and driveways in the not too distant future!

Must go now and brush-up on it

November

For the past few nights I have listened to the Fallow bucks who, with their guttural, rutting grunts, have been making their presence known to all and sundry. This eerie sound together with the occasional clashing of antlers has disturbed the peaceful sleep of the Forest and all its inhabitants. But the bucks are not the only culprits who are causing distress to the resting Forest. Just the other night I was standing in a grassy ride minding my own business when across the still air came the sound of several voices and as I searched the darkness for the source of this disturbance I was amazed to see several huge, bright lights bobbing toward me. I stood and watched as these alien illuminations turned across the track and off through the trees. I was somewhat comforted in the sure knowledge that visitors from outer space would not be speaking English nor would they be riding mountain bikes; for this is what they were – an organised group of mountain bikers and I counted more than fifty of them as they passed by, oblivious to the fact that they were being watched. Now I am a fairly liberal sort of chap and if riding on the Forest in the pitch darkness rattles your cage then carry on and do it, as far as I know it's not illegal. But what does contravene Forest bylaws is the riding of bicycles anywhere other than on the 100 miles or more of marked, gravelled tracks and, by the way, this bylaw has not been put in place to spoil people's enjoyment but essentially to protect this very fragile environment. Clearly the thoughtless organisers of these events (and I'm advised that my sighting was not a one-off) have little or no respect for our Forest and I'm sure that they cannot comprehend the damage that such outings can cause. More to the point, after a day of dodging tourists, horse riders, dog walkers, forest workers, etc., surely the rightful inhabitants of the Forest are entitled to a little peace and quiet – aren't they?

At this time of the year some newcomers to the Forest are often puzzled by roadside signs which warn the motorist that a roundup is taking place. These roundups are known locally as drifts and they are conducted by bone-fide Commoners under the supervision of the Agisters who are, in turn, appointed and employed by the Verderers. Drifts take place in various locations in the Forest and their purpose is to drive the ponies into corrals or pounds so that they may be wormed, tail-marked (to show that their owner has paid his fee), branded and, in more recent years, fitted with a fluorescent collar in an attempt to reduce the numbers of road traffic accidents.

It is, without doubt, a truly magnificent and unique sight to see these expert riders in their leather chaps working their way through the thick gorse as they cleverly funnel the wild ponies into the pounds but, if you want to watch, then watch from afar. Wild ponies are unpredictable and the Commoners have a difficult job as it is without the added responsibility of watching out for the safety of inexperienced sightseers. This is a serious and necessary operation for the Commoners and without the drifts their way of life would be impossible and without the Commoners ponies the Forest would revert to wild scrub land and the neatly mown verges and lawns that epitomise our Forest would be a thing of the past. Oh, and by the way, if you want to take some photos I'm sure you'll have the good manners to ask their permission first!

Must go now before you drift-off too!

December

The Christmas carol *'The Holly and the Ivy'* is one of the many, long-standing traditions of Christmas. But how did these and other time-honoured plants from the countryside, such as mistletoe, become so deeply ingrained into our December festivities?

The ancient Romans, it seems, decorated their temples and homes with greenery and flowers to celebrate the rebirth of the year. This festival of Saturnalia lasted a week from 17th December to 23rd December and was the largest festival in the Roman calendar with much eating and drinking and relaxation of social rules. Slaves were given time to themselves and the giving of gifts was a common event during this period. Other early European, tribal cultures celebrated the Winter Solstice (the shortest day of the year) on 21st December with gargantuan feasts in recognition of the end of the long dark days of early winter and to pay tribute to the sun for the welcome return of the longer, lighter days that were to come. One doesn't need too much imagination to realise just how miraculous these evergreen shrubs must have seemed to these early people for, when every tree or bush was laid bare and frost or snow was the order of the day, the spirit of these primitive souls must have been at its lowest ebb. Their hopes must have been raised, however, by the sight of the holly, with its succulent green leaves and vibrant red berries, growing alongside the heart shaped leaves of the climbing ivy with its clusters of nectar-ladened flowers; whilst, higher up in the barren canopy, the green mistletoe with its waxy, white berries stood out proudly against the grey, winter sky. It's no wonder, therefore, that our forebears were convinced that such plants must have been possessed of miraculous powers and they became the symbols of eternal life and continuing renewal.

Holly was traditionally thought of as a 'male' plant, probably because of its prickly leaves. Ivy, on the other hand, with its heart-shaped leaves and clinging, climbing nature was considered to be a 'female' plant. Holly and ivy were combined in decoration to represent the union between men and women. But care in their use was essential for it was considered unlucky if holly or ivy were brought over the threshold before Christmas Eve and, whichever was brought into the house first, i.e. the man or the woman, would dictate the house rules for the coming year! It was also considered unlucky to take down these green decorations before

Candlemas Eve (1st February). However, if you were unlucky enough to be troubled by house goblins, it was permissible to hang a bunch of holly in your house for the remainder of the year in order to keep the little varmints at bay.

From early times mistletoe has been revered as one of the most magical of plants.

Holly

Branches of mistletoe were hung from doors and ceilings to ward off evil spirits and to prevent the entrance of witches and in later times it became a symbol of peace under which warring enemies could call a truce and feuding spouses could kiss and make-up.

The custom of kissing under the mistletoe is thought to date back to the good old Saturnalian revelries but like the aforementioned holly and ivy we must be careful to stick to the correct etiquette. Once a man has

kissed a woman under the mistletoe he should pluck a berry from the branch and, when all the berries are gone, sadly, the kissing must stop – so make sure you get a branch with lots of berries. Furthermore, the Christmas mistletoe should be burned on the Twelfth Night or the men and women who have kissed under it may never marry.

Miseltoe

Somewhere around the 4th century the Christians decided to instigate the festival of Christmas and not wishing to come up against too much opposition from their new converts they deliberately chose a date that would be compatible with both Saturnalia and the Winter Solstice. It is not surprising therefore that many of the old myths and traditions survive in the modern day Christmas festivities.

Have a merry Christmas, but do be careful.

The other books From a New Forest Inclosure

From A New Forest Inclosure
The First Two Years
Ian Thew

From a New Forest Inclosure
Book Two 2006 & 2007
Ian Tew

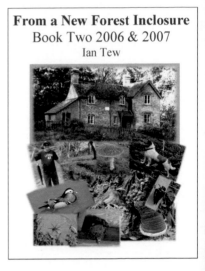

From a New Forest Inclosure
Book Three 2008 & 2009
Ian Thew

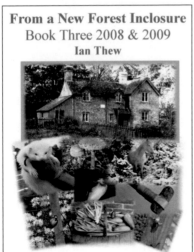

From A New Forest Inclosure
Book Four 2010 & 2011
Ian Thew

These books are available by post: Please send £5,99 per book plus £2.50 postage and packaging (up to four books) to Ian Thew, Burley Rails Cottage, Burley BH24 4HT England Or telephone 01425 403735 with your name, postal address and card details. Email ian@ithew.freeserve.co.uk

Burley Rails Cottage, Wilfs Cabin and Paddocks

Wilfs Cabin

Stables

Wilfs Cabin; a self-contained, snug, traditional log cabin that provides a double bed room with en-suite shower, a cosy lounge and a galley kitchen. The timbered veranda is ideal for alfresco dining or for just relaxing with a glass of wine after a busy day in the Forest.

For the four legged visitors there are two, modern, block-built, stables with individual yards and a tack room with all facilities, which are adjacent to two small turn-out paddocks. There is ample parking and undercover storage for traps and bikes.

www.burleyrailscottage.co.uk   Tel:01425 403735

Well behaved and sociable dogs are also welcome.

NEWFOREST
Shooting & Fishing | Coaching & Tuition

The New Forest Fly Fishing and Shooting School was founded by Ian Thew who lives deep in the heart of the New Forest which is situated on the South Coast between the mighty rivers Test and Avon and offers the ultimate in fishing and shooting possibilities.

Our objective is to provide the very best in fly fishing and clay and game shooting for both the complete novice or the experienced sportsman and to this end we extend the opportunity to learn new skills or to hone existing expertise over a wide range of disciplines.

We take pride in providing instruction and coaching in all aspects of fishing and shooting to the very highest of standards and we take care to ensure that when our pupils leave us they will have been well versed in both safety and etiquette and will thus be able to move on in their selected sport with personal assurance and confidence.

Ian Thew is a qualified fly fishing coach and a qualified shooting instructor and, in addition to running the New Forest Fly Fishing and Shooting School, he writes regular features on all aspects of shooting, fishing and country sports related topics for magazines such as the Shooting Times and the Countrymans' weekly.

Ian is also a qualified deer stalker and over the past forty years he has amassed a unique and widespread knowledge of most rural activities from fishing to ferreting and just about everything else in between.

Contact Ian on 01425 403735
ian@ithew.freeserve.co.uk

www.shootingandfishingcoaching.co.uk